TEXAS
JURISPRUDENCE
STUDY GUIDE

TEXAS
JURISPRUDENCE STUDY GUIDE

VASILIOS A. ZERRIS MD, MPH, MSc
GERHARD FRIEHS, MD
HOWARD SMITH, MD, JD

Copyright © 2012 by Vasilios A. Zerris Inc. Boston, MA

Library of Congress Control Number:		2011913433
ISBN:	Hardcover	978-1-4653-4388-8
	Softcover	978-1-4653-4387-1
	Ebook	978-1-4653-4389-5

All rights reserved. No part of this book may be reproduced or transmitted in any form or by any means, electronic or mechanical, including photocopying, recording, or by any information storage and retrieval system, without permission in writing from the copyright owner.

This book was printed in the United States of America.

To order additional copies of this book, contact:
Xlibris Corporation
1-888-795-4274
www.Xlibris.com
Orders@Xlibris.com
95438

CONTENTS

Chapter 1	Civil Liability	11
Chapter 2	Drugs and Prescribing	23
Chapter 3	Confidentiality	37
Chapter 4	Regulation of the Practice of Medicine	49
Chapter 5	Business Organizations in Health Care	81
Chapter 6	Fraud and Abuse	85
Chapter 7	Credentialing and Peer Review	91
Chapter 8	Consent, Patient Rights, and Advanced Directives	97
Chapter 9	Birth and Death	115
Chapter 10	Reporting Requirements in Suspected Abuse or Neglect	137
Chapter 11	Disease Prevention, Control, and Reporting	147
Chapter 12	Mental Health and Chemical Dependency	157
Chapter 13	Emergency Medical Treatment and Hospital Transfers	165
Chapter 14	Numbers, Dates, Times to Remember	173

Dedications

I dedicate this book to my father, Athanasios Zerris MD, and my mother, Anna Zerris, who are the two most wonderful and kind people I know.

> Vasilios A. Zerris MD, MPH, MSc
> Neurosurgeon

I dedicate this book to my wife Laura for her ongoing support and love.

> Howard Smith MD, JD
> Neurosurgeon

I dedicate this book to my children, who serve as an inspiration for me every day.

> Gerhard Friehs MD
> Neurosurgeon

Foreword

The medical and legal systems have become increasingly intertwined. The goal of this book is two-fold. First, to present the high yield facts in a concise and systematic manner that will allow busy medical professionals to efficiently and effectively prepare for the jurisprudence exam required for medical licensing in Texas. Secondly, to familiarize healthcare personnel with the basic legal issues they may encounter in their day-to-day medical practice.

The book has been formatted to allow for easy studying, memorization, and self-testing. The left side of each page contains the question and the right side contains the answers and legal references.

Vasilios A. Zerris MD, MPH, MSc

Chapter 1

Civil Liability

Can a patient successfully sue a doctor if there is no physician-patient relationship?	**No** (*Lection v. Dyll*, 65 SW 3d 696, 704 (Tex App.—Dallas, pet. denied)).
If there is no prior physician-patient relationship, are you legally obliged to respond to a call from a patient for treatment?	**No** (*Salas v. Gamboa*, 760 SW 2d 838, 841 (Tex. App.—San Antonio 1988, no writ)).
Does being on call give rise to a physician-patient relationship?	**No** (*Mazjoub v. Appling*, 95 SW 3d 432, 438 (Tex. App.—Houston [1st Dist.] 2002, pet. denied)).
How can one terminate a physician-patient relationship, without abandonment if there is ongoing treatment?	**30 days written notice, must provide for emergency** (*King v. Fisher*, 918 SW 2d 108, 112 (Tex. App.—Fort Worth 1996, writ denied)).

Does a physician's duty extend to the unborn child or potential victims of an ill patient?	**Yes** (*Gooden v. Tips*, 651 SW 2d 364, 365 (Tex. App.—Tyler 1983, no writ)).
What is "proximate cause"?	**Prove that negligence caused harm and that the cause was not too remote; what is required to hold a defendant liable in a civil lawsuit** (*Rehabilitation Care Sys. of Am. v. Davis*, 43 SW 3d 649, 660-662 (Tex. App.—Texarkana 2001, pet. denied)).
What are the two components of proximate cause?	**Cause-in-fact (but-for test) and foreseeability** (*Columbia Medical Center of Las Colinas v. A. Hona Hogue*, 271 SW 3d 238, 244, 2008.).
Does an expert witness have to 1. be actively practicing medicine? 2. know standards of care? 3. have enough training to express an opinion on whether standard of care was provided? 4. be board certified?	 Yes. Yes. Yes. **No, has to be board certified OR EQUIVALENT** (Tex. Civ. Prac. & Rem. Code Ann. §74.401-.403).

In a medical malpractice case, are expert witnesses required?	**Yes, with two exceptions** (*Spinks v. Brown*, 103 SW 3d 452 (Tex. App.—San Antonio 2002, pet. denied)).
In a medical malpractice setting, what 2 instances do not need expert testimony?	**Res ipsa loquitur (e.g., amputation of wrong leg) and negligence per se (a law was broken)** (Tex. Civ. Prac. & Rem. Code Ann. §74.201; *Ridgecrest Ret. & Healthcare v. Urban*, 135 SW 3d 757, 762-763 (Tex. App.—Houston [1st Dist.] 2004, pet. denied)).
What are "exemplary damages"?	**Damages above compensatory designed to punish the defendant and deter the behavior** (Tex. Civ. Prac. & Rem. Code §§41.001(7), 41.001(11), 41.001-.003).
When do you award them?	**To punish and deter defendant** (Tex. Civ. Prac. & Rem. Code §§41.001(7), 41.001(11), 41.001-.003).
Is there a cap to noneconomic damages? How much?	**$250,000 for physicians, $500,000 for hospitals** (Tex. Civ. Prac. & Rem. Code §74.301-.302).

Does this cap depend on the number of defendants or claimants?	**No** (Tex. Civ. Prac. & Rem. Code §74.301-.302).
What is "proportional responsibility"?	**Percentage of liability apportioned according to percentage of fault** (Tex. Civ. Prac. & Rem. Code §33.001-.017).
Can the claimant have part of the proportional responsibility?	**Yes** (Tex. Civ. Prac. & Rem. Code §33.003(a)).
If the claimant's proportionate responsibility is more than what %, he/she may not recover damages?	**If > 50%, no damages awarded** (Tex. Civ. Prac. & Rem. Code §§33.001; 33.012(a); 33.012(d)).
How long is the statute of limitations for adults? For minors?	**2 years; for minors 2 years after becoming 18 years of age** (Tex. Civ. Prac. & Rem. Code §74.251).
By how much can this be extended and how?	**File complaint—extra 60-day, notice letter extends statute by 75 days** (Tex. Civ. Prac. & Rem. Code §74.251).
What is the statute of limitations for wrongful death?	**2 years** (*Russell v. Ingersoll Rand Co.*, 841 SW 2d 343, 345 (Tex. 1992)).

What is the discovery rule? Give examples.	**Statute does not begin until damage is discovered. For example, a retained sponge that is found 3 years post-op** (*Shah v. Moss*, 67 SW 3d 836, 842 (Tex. 2001)).
Is there immunity from civil action in emergency cases?	**Yes, except gross negligence** (Tex. Civ. Prac. & Rem. Code §74.151).
Is there immunity from civil action in volunteer care?	**Yes, except gross negligence** (Tex. Civ. Prac. & Rem. Code §84.004(c)).
When can a physician be charged with "assault and battery"?	**Un-consented surgery or examination or when exceeding the scope of the consent** (*Miller v. HCA, Inc.*, 118 SW 3d, 758 (Tex. 2003)).
When can a physician be charged with patient abandonment?	**Unilateral cessation of treatment when continued treatment is necessary** (*King v. Fisher*, 918 SW 2d 108, 112 (Tex. App.—Fort Worth 1996, writ denied)).
What is "strict liability"?	**Liability that does not depend on actual negligence, but that is based on a breach of a duty to make something safe. This often applies to product liability** (*Black's Law Dictionary*, 9th Ed., B. A. Gardner, Edit., 2009, p. 998).

Are hospitals liable for the actions of a physician?	**No, unless the hospital employs the physician** (*Baptist Memorial Hospital System v. Sampson*, 969 SW 2d 945, 948 (Tex. 1998)).
Who determines in a criminal case if the medical records of a patient should be released?	**Judge by inspection** (Tex. R. Evid. 509 and 510; MPA §159.003(a) (10)).
How many days do you have to release medical records to an attorney?	**45 days** (Tex. Civ. Prac. & Rem. Code §74.051(d)).
Can medical records be admitted as evidence in court? What are the requirements?	**Yes, but only with affidavit** (Tex. R. Evid. 803(6)).

Chapter 2

Drugs and Prescribing

What are schedule 1, 2, 3, 4, 5 drugs?	Schedule 1—no known use (e.g., heroin); schedule 2—very addictive (morphine, cocaine); schedule 3-5—less addictive (Texas Health & Safety Code §481.001-.205).
What are dangerous drugs?	Prescription drugs other than schedule 1-5 (Texas Health & Safety Code §483.001(2)).
How many DEA registrations do you need if you prescribe drugs? dispense drugs?	One to prescribe; a separate registration for each location where you dispense (21 CFR §1301.12).
How often do you renew your DEA license?	Every 3 years (21 CFR §1301.13.).

TEXAS JURISPRUDENCE STUDY GUIDE

Can you move your office location and then change your DEA?	**No, need to change BEFORE move** (21 CFR §1301.51).
Is a DEA registration sufficient to prescribe drugs in Texas?	**No, also need Department of Public Safety Bureau of Narcotics and Dangerous Drug registration** (Texas Health & Safety Code §§481.061(c), 481.063(g)).
How often do you renew a DPS license?	**Yearly** (Texas Health & Safety Code §§481.061(c), 481.063(g)).
Do you have to display the DEA and DPS licenses?	**Not required by any statute.**
How many days do you have to notify the DPS of any change in your information (name, address, tel., etc.)?	**7 days** (37 Tex. Admin. Code 13.208.).
Can you have your DPS suspended and keep your DEA or vice versa?	**No, they are interconnected** (21 USCA §824; Texas Health & Safety Code §§481.063(e), 481.066).
For schedules 2-5 drugs, can you just put the number of pills on prescription?	**No, number and number spelled out** (21 CFR §1306.05; Texas Health & Safety Code §481.074(k)).

Do you have to put intended use on prescription?	**Yes** (21 CFR §1306.05; Texas Health & Safety Code §481.074(k)).
With how many days of a schedule 2-5 drug can a patient be discharged from the hospital?	**7 days but only if drug was already prescribed in the hospital** (Texas Health & Safety Code §481.074(j)).
What kind of prescription pad do you need for schedule 2 drugs? Can you use stickers?	**Official DPS form, no stickers** (Texas Health & Safety Code §481.075(a)).
Can a physician prescribe schedule 2 over the phone, and what is the procedure?	**Yes, for emergencies and only for the duration of emergency** (21 CFR §1306.11(d); Texas Health & Safety Code §481.074(b)).
How many days does the physician have to mail the schedule's emergency prescription to the pharmacy?	**7 days** (21 CFR §1306.11(d); Texas Health & Safety Code §481.074(b)).
How many days does the patient have to fill schedule 2 prescriptions?	**7 days** (21 CFR §1306.12; Texas Health & Safety Code §481.074(d)).
Can you refill a schedule 2 prescription? How about schedule 3-5?	**No refills for schedule 2; maximum 5 refills for schedules 3-5** (21 CFR §§1306.12; 1306.22; Texas Health & Safety Code §§481.074(d), 481.074(h)).

TEXAS JURISPRUDENCE STUDY GUIDE

Who can call in prescription from a physician's office?	**Any qualified DESIGNATED person** (Texas Health & Safety Code §§481.073; 483.001(4) 483.022, 483.041-.042; Tex. Admin. Code §13.205).
Can they call in schedule 2?	**Only physician in emergencies** (21 CFR §1306.11(d); Texas Health & Safety Code §481.074(b)).
Can a physician prohibit substitutions for generics?	**Yes** (Tex. Occ. Code §562.015; Tex. Admin. Code §309.3-.4).
From whom and how do you order schedule 2? Schedules 3-5?	**Schedule 2 on triplicate order form from distributor; schedules 3-5 regular form from wholesaler** (21 USCA §828; 21 CFR §1305.01-.16; Texas Health & Safety Code §481.069).
What drugs do you need to keep records on? How are the records kept? How often do you need to do inventory? Do you need to submit the records? How long do you have to keep the last inventory list?	**If dispensed in office, then all dangerous drugs, schedule drugs and samples; separate records for schedule 1+2; inventory every 2 years; records are not submitted; keep records for 2 years** (21 USCA §827; 21 CFR §1304.03-.04; Texas Health & Safety Code §§481.067, 483.023-.025; MPA §164.053; 37 Tex. Admin. Code §13.201-.209).

29

TEXAS JURISPRUDENCE STUDY GUIDE

Who can inspect your drugs?	**TMB, DPS, attorney general for the DEA** (Texas Health & Safety Code §483.023-.025).
What is the method of ordering and accounting for drug samples?	**Written and signed request by physician; must keep inventory and drug logs** (MPA §158.002).
Can you repackage samples?	**No** (MPA §158.002).
Do you need to keep records on samples?	**Yes, just like other meds** (MPA §158.002).
Can a physician buy and rebottle? Any exceptions?	**No, except for rural areas (less than 5000 population of town or 2500 of municipality, closest pharmacy > 15 miles)** (MPA §158.003).
To give anesthesia, how often do you have to register with the board?	**Every 2 years** (22 Tex. Admin. Code §192.1-.6).
What life support competency do surgeons and anesthesiologists need?	**ACLS, PALS, or board-approved course** (22 Tex. Admin. Code §192.1-.6).

TEXAS JURISPRUDENCE STUDY GUIDE

How many and what competency levels of healthcare providers do you need in all settings?	**At least 2 physicians with advanced competency** (22 Tex. Admin. Code §192.1-.6.).
How many days do you have to report office-based anesthesia-related complications?	**15 days** (22 Tex. Admin. Code §192.1-.6).
What is considered an anesthesia-related complication?	**Admission to hospital within 24 hours or death within 72 hours** (22 Tex. Admin. Code §192.1-.6).
What is considered intractable pain?	**Pain where cause of pain cannot be removed and where relief or cure has not been found** (Tex. Occ. Code §107.001-.152).
Can a hospital forbid a physician to give dangerous drugs or controlled substances for treatment of intractable pain?	**No** (Tex. Occ. Code §107.001-.152).
Can the board take disciplinary action against a physician for giving dangerous or controlled substances to a patient with intractable pain?	**No** (Tex. Occ. Code §107.001-.152).

What must the physician document prior to treatment of intractable pain?	**Understanding between physician and patient about treatment; dose, type, frequency of medication; consultation with psychologist, psychiatrist, addictions expert** (Tex. Occ. Code §107.001-.152).
Can you guarantee that a drug will work?	**No** (Texas Health & Safety Code §431.021).

Chapter 3

CONFIDENTIALITY

Who can be part of a confidential communication?	**Persons involved, furthering interest of the patient, and those participating in diagnosis or treatment, e.g., patients, doctors, translators, nurses, etc** (MPA §159.001-.002; Tex. R. Evid. 509).
Is the billing record confidential?	**No, billing record is NOT part of medical record** (MPA §159.004).
In a criminal proceeding, is the physician-patient privilege communication confidential?	**NO (except for mental health records); judicial ruling should be obtained** (Tex. R. Evid. 509 and 510; MPA §159.003(a) (10)).
In a criminal proceeding, are records of alcohol and drug abuse confidential?	**Yes** (Tex. R. Evid. 509 and 510; MPA §159.003(a) (10)).

Does the physician confidentiality apply to court or administrative proceedings brought by the patient against a physician?	**No** (MPA §159.003).
Can the physician violate confidentiality if he/she thinks he or someone else is in danger?	**Yes, must report that to law enforcement agency (NOT for mental health)** (MPA §159.004).
What information must a release of medical records include?	**Type of records, reason, and person to whom to release** (Tex. R. Evid. 509; MPA §159.005).
How many days (hospital) or business days (physician) does a hospital/physician have to provide medical records when they are requested?	**Physician has 15 business days, hospital has 15 days** (MPA §159.006; 22 Tex. Admin. Code §165.2).
What is "therapeutic privilege," when can it be used, who has access to the information, and what is the protocol the physician must follow?	**If physician thinks that information would be harmful to the patient, it can be withheld; in writing, copy in the chart; films or tests must be released to patient representative** (MPA §159.006).

TEXAS JURISPRUDENCE STUDY GUIDE

Can the physician charge for medical records and films? For an affidavit? Does he have to give the information if the patient does not pay? What does he do if the patient does not pay?	**Yes, can charge $25 for first 20 pages, then 15¢ per page plus postage; notarization $15, films $8; patient MUST pay to get records, 10-day notice** (MPA §159.007).
Can you charge a patient requesting records in order to apply for disability or public aid? How many copies are patients entitled to? Can you charge if federal agency is requesting records?	**No; one copy; no** (Texas Health & Safety Code §161.201-.204).
How many years does a physician MD have to keep records for adults? for minors? How many years do hospitals have to keep records for adults? For minors?	**7 years for adults, 7 years or until age 21; hospital 10 years** (22 Tex. Admin. Code §165.1; Texas Health & Safety Code §241.103.).
Can a physician or hospital get rid of records after the required years if these records might be part of a litigation?	**No** (22 Tex. Admin. Code §165.1).
Can you relate information without patient consent for treatment? Billing? To report abuse? To law enforcement? For funeral directions? For worker's comp?	**Yes, all of above** (Texas Health & Safety Code §§181.052-.055; .057-.058.).

What is the "minimum necessary standard" for a medical release?	**It protects health care information unless it is required to be released (investigation, law enforcement, authorized release, participating care providers, HIPAA compliant release)** (45 CFR §164.502(b)(1)).
Does a patient have the right to see his/her own record? Can he/she ask for amendments to the records?	**Yes; yes, they can request amendments** (45 CFR §164.524(a)(1); 45 CFR §164.526).
What is the Texas medical record privacy act? Is it like HIPAA?	**It is the state equivalent of HIPAA** (Texas Health & Safety Code §181.001 et seq.).
Within how many days must a hospital send an itemized bill to patients? Is this mandatory? Or done by request? When must the hospital inform patients of this option?	**Upon request, within 30 business days; hospital must inform patient of availability of itemized bill** (Texas Health & Safety Code §311.002(b)).
Can medical records be obtained with a subpoena? Does this include substance-abuse records?	**Yes; no** (Tex. R. Evid. 509 and 510; MPA §159.003(a)(10); 42 CFR §213(b)).
Are substance abuse records admissible during criminal proceedings?	**No, unless the crime is EXTREMELY serious** (42 CFR §2.65(d)).

Is HIV information confidential?	**Yes** (Texas Health & Safety Code §81.101-.104).
Can you "break" confidentiality in order to tell a spouse that his/her spouse is HIV positive?	**Yes** (Texas Health & Safety Code §81.101-.104).
Can you break confidentiality to tell a partner about notification program?	**Yes** (Texas Health & Safety Code §81.101-.104).
Are blood bank records confidential?	**Yes** (Texas Health & Safety Code §162.001-.015.).
If a blood bank finds a donor with an infectious disease, can they call other blood banks and tell them the name of donor and the disease?	**They can tell name of donor, NOT disease** (Texas Health & Safety Code §162.001-.015).
If a blood bank finds that blood outbound to hospitals is HIV positive, can they call the hospitals and give name of donor? Type of disease?	**They can tell name of disease, NOT donor** (Texas Health & Safety Code §162.001-.015).
For statistical purposes, can a blood bank give out medical records? Names?	**Yes, but not names or other identifying information** (Texas Health & Safety Code §162.001-.015).

Is genetic information confidential?	**Yes** (Texas Labor Code §21.401-.405 (employers); Tex. Rev. Civ. Stat., art. 9031(licensing authorities); and Tex. Ins. Code §546.001-.152 (issuers of group health benefit plans)).
Can patients have access to the results of their genetic testing?	**Yes** (Texas Labor Code §21.401-.405 (employers); Tex. Rev. Civ. Stat., art. 9031 (licensing authorities); and Tex. Ins. Code §546.001-.152 (issuers of group health benefit plans)).
What kind of crime is the unauthorized release of records?	**Misdemeanor** (42 USC §290dd-2; 42 CFR §2.4).

Chapter 4

REGULATION OF THE PRACTICE OF MEDICINE

Can the Texas Medical Board (TMB) show preference to a specific school of medicine such as medicine v. osteopathy?	**NO** (Texas Constitution, art. XVI, §31).
What does the Medical Practice Act (MPA) regulate?	**The practice of medicine** (MPA §151.003).
Who does the MPA apply to?	**Physicians (MD, DO), PAs, and acupuncturists** (MPA §§151.001-165.160).
Does the MPA apply to the armed forces and federal public health? Can they moonlight?	**It does NOT apply to a federal job, they can NOT moonlight outside the federal setting** (MPA §151.052(a) 8).

TEXAS JURISPRUDENCE STUDY GUIDE

Does the MPA apply to emergency assistance if there is NO charge of money? If there is money charged or billed?	**NO if no charge; YES if money is charged** (MPA §151.052(a) 9).
Are medical students in "board-approved schools" subject to the MPA?	**NO** (MPA §151.052(a) 10).
Does the MPA prohibit self-care?	**NO** (MPA §151.054).
Does the MPA apply to physicians in contiguous states?	**NO (physicians from nearby states can only order care for patients in hospice or nursing homes)** (MPA §151.056).
How many people are on the TMB? Who appoints them? Who must confirm them?	**19 members, appointed by the governor, confirmed by the senate** (MPA §152.002-.005).
Can the board subpoena people and records? Who can serve a subpoena?	**YES, subpoenas can be served by board investigator or sent by certified mail** (MPA §153.007).
How often does the Department of Public Safety (DPS; state police) check on physicians and report to the board?	**Quarterly** (Tex. Code Crim. Proc., art. 60-061).

What are acceptable methods to tell the public on how to register a complaint to the TMB? In what languages? Where can a physician include this info?	**By phone (direct number and 1-800 number) or by mail; posted sign, on registration forms or bill; in English and Spanish** (MPA §154.051; 22 Tex. Admin. Code §178.3).
How often must the TMB disseminate updated information? What info is included?	**2 times per year; info includes disciplinary action, board activities and functions, changes to the MPA and attorney general opinions** (MPA §154.003).
Are disciplinary orders private or public?	**Public** (MPA §154.004).
Are the following included in the physician profile? 1. ethnic origin 2. CME 3. years in practice 4. Medicaid participation 5. misdemeanors 6. felonies 7. malpractice claims 8. tax ID or social security numbers	**Everything except for tax ID/ soc. security** (MPA §154.006; 22 Tex. Admin. Code §173, et seq.).
Which malpractice claims should be included?	**Any jury awards, liabilities– NOT settlements** (MPA §154.006; 22 Tex. Admin. Code §173).

What happens if you don't give this info?	**License is not renewed** (22 Tex. Admin. Code §173.2).
How many years of postgraduate training do you need to be eligible for licensure?	**One** (MPA §155.003).
Who can get a limited license?	**Applicant who is recommended by dean, president, or chief administrator from Texas medical school** (MPA §155.006).
Do you need the jurisprudence exam for a limited license?	**Yes** (MPA §155.006).
Who is not eligible for licensure?	**If applicant is under prosecution, investigation, or has restrictions on license in another state** (MPA §155.003(e)).
How many days does the program director have to tell the board that somebody with a physician-in-training license did not show up, was suspended, etc.?	**30 days** (MPA §171.6).
What is a temporary postgraduate training permit?	**License for residents and fellows pending the physician in training permit** (22 Tex. Admin. Code §171.3).

What is a telemedicine license? Do you have to be board certified to have it? Do you have to pass the jurisprudence exam?	**A license to do consulting work through internet, etc., in Texas; cannot physically see or treat patients; board certification is required; JP exam required** (22 Tex. Admin. Code §172.12-.15).
How often do you register your license? Do you need an updated physician profile?	**Every 2 years; yes** (MPA §156.001).
How many days prior to the expiration of your license does the TMB notify you?	**30** (MPA §156.004).
Expired licenses: 1. How many days after a license expires are you considered to be practicing without a license? 2. License expired < 90 days—penalty is? 3. License expired 91-364 days—penalty is? 4. License expired > 364 days—penalty is? 5. Do you have to retake JP exam if your license is canceled?	(MPA §156.004-.005) **30 day grace period.** **US$75.** **US$150.** **License canceled.** **Only if the license is canceled for more than 2 years.**
How can you get another license if it is lost/destroyed?	**Get affidavit of lost or destroyed document and pay fee to board** (MPA §155.151).

How many CMEs per year?	**24** (MPA §156.051 et seq.; 22 Tex. Admin. Code 166.2).
1. How many category 1?	**12.**
2. How many category 1 must be in ethics?	**1.**
3. How many category 2 can be from volunteer work?	**6 hours.**
4. How many CMEs can a license carry forward? and for how many registration periods?	**48; only once.**
5. How many CMEs can be applied retroactively?	**24, only once.**
6. How many CMEs do you need if you become "board certified" within 36 months?	**24.**
7. If you practice pain management, how many CMEs in pain management are required?	**None, but they are recommended.**
Who can initiate a complaint?	**Anyone** (MPA §154.051).
What is the "health professions council"?	**Council of various professionals that establishes a central telephone complaint system (800-number)** (Tex. Occ. Code §101.001 et seq.).

Does the TMB have to notify a physician when a complaint is filed? Are there exceptions? How often do the parties get updated on proceedings?	**Yes, within 30 days, except if it would interfere with the investigation; updates are quarterly** (MPA §154.053).
When does the TMB release complaint information to the hospital?	**Upon written request** (MPA §154.054).
Who investigates issues of "medical competency"?	**An expert physician panel appointed by the board consisting of physicians ONLY** (MPA §154.058).
What do medical malpractice carriers have to report to the TMB regarding malpractice? Within what time limit? Who punishes them if they do not report? What does a physician without insurance have to report and when? Is there a difference for NPDB/HCQIA?	**Within 30 days from a complaint being filed in a lawsuit, settlement; noninsured MDs have to self-report within 30 days; any payment must be reported to NPDB by HCQIA requirements** (MPA §160.051 et seq.; 22 Tex. Admin. Code §176.1 et seq.).

Restrictive action by the TMB: 1. Within what time limit must the board tell the hospital? Tell Medicare? Tell the secretary of health & professional societies & complainant? 2. How often must the board make public notices about disciplinary orders? 3. Must the board report crimes found during investigations? 4. Within how many days must the board report to the NPDB? 5. Within how many days must a court report to the board about convictions, felonies, and misdemeanors and addiction issues be filed?	(MPA §164.060; MPA §154.003; MPA §160.051 et seq.) **Next working day for hospitals; in writing for all within 30 days.** **2 times per year.** **Yes, to the law enforcement.** **30 days.** **30 days.**
Are TMB reports confidential?	**Yes** (MPA §160.005).
Who can the NPDB give info to? How about to patients? How about statistical data?	**Hospitals, self-requesting physicians, board, other state or federal agencies, attorneys; for statistical purposes if no identity disclosed** (45 CFR §60.11).

TEXAS JURISPRUDENCE STUDY GUIDE

When is it not illegal to perform a third-trimester abortion?	**To prevent mother's death, if unborn has severe irreversible brain damage** (Texas Health & Safety Code §170.002).
When is it not illegal to perform an abortion on a minor?	**In emergency and with court order** (Tex. Fam. Code §33.002).
Is sexual contact between a physician and patient OK if the patient consents?	**NO, the disparity of power does not allow consent** (MPA §164.053; 22 Tex. Admin. Code §190.8(2)).
Why is it unprofessional to initially prescribe drugs over the Internet?	**Did not verify identity of patient, no physician coverage or follow-up guaranteed** (22 Tex. Admin. Code §190.8(1)).
How can you terminate care to a patient?	**30 day notice, certified letter, available for emergencies during that time, give alternative physicians** (22 Tex. Admin. Code §190.8(1)).

What prescriptions does a physician need to keep records on? Dangerous drugs? Controlled substances? Samples?	**Samples and dangerous drugs as part of medical record; for schedule 3-5 records and log; for schedule 2 separate log and records; keep record for 2 years; do inventory on schedule drugs every 2 years** (MPA §164.054).
Can the board administer monetary penalties?	**Yes** (MPA §164.001).
What happens to his/her license if a physician goes to prison?	**TMB is required to suspend** (MPA §164.057).
How many malpractice claims within what time period automatically open a board investigation?	**3 within 5 years** (MPA §164.201; Tex. Admin. Code §176.8).
How many people from the TMB are necessary to temporarily suspend a license?	**President appoints a 3-member panel; can be done by phone** (MPA §164.059; 22 Tex. Admin. Code §187.55-.62).
Is self-reporting addiction a disciplinary action? Is a rehabilitation order a disciplinary order?	**No; no, it is the only nondisciplinary order** (MPA §164.202-.204).

Is probation a disciplinary order? Who cannot be put on probation?	**Yes; sex offenders, felons, prisoners, or if the physician is a threat to public** (MPA §164.101-.103).
Can the TMB make a physician give a refund? What is the maximum amount of refund?	**Yes; cannot be more than the amount paid** (MPA §164.206).
What is monitoring?	**Continued oversight of the board for subjects on disciplinary orders** (MPA §164.010).
Who is part of an informal hearing and what is it?	**Members of the board, at least one of whom is a public member, physician, his/her attorney; a means to settle a case without an administrative hearing** (MPA §164.003; 22 Tex. Admin. Code §187.00 et seq.).
When do you go to formal hearings? What is the SOAH? Is it part of the TMB? Who holds the hearings? Who is participating? Must the TMB follow the ruling of the administrative law judge?	**If no settlement reached after informal hearing; state office of administrative hearing; no; board members, physician, attorneys, and administrative law judge; NO, they do not have to follow the judge's ruling** (MPA §164.007; 22 Tex. Admin. Code §187.22-.42).

Where can a physician file an appeal? Within what time period? Can he practice in the interim?	**Circuit court Travis county, within 30 days after final board decision; physician cannot practice in interim** (MPA §164.009-.011).
Can the TMB panel serve a subpoena to a physician?	**Yes** (MPA §153.007).
Can the physician get his file?	**Yes, with written request, within 30 days** (MPA §164.007(d)).
Can you voluntarily surrender your license?	**Yes, but board does not have to accept it** (MPA §164.001).
If you surrender your license to avoid disciplinary action, can you reapply for it?	**Yes, if there is no prohibitive circumstance** (22 Tex. Admin. Code §196.2).
If you surrender your license voluntarily, whose burden is it to show competence if you want it back?	**The physician who surrendered the license** (22 Tex. Admin. Code §196.4-.5).
How often and how soon can you reapply to have your license reinstated if it has been canceled/suspended, etc.?	**Once a year** (MPA §164.151-.154).

What is the maximum administrative penalty? How long do you have to pay it?	**$5000 per violation; 30 days** (MPA §165.003; MPA §165.005).
What is the maximum penalty for an action for civil penalty by the attorney general? How long do you have to pay it?	**$1000 per penalty, 30 days** (MPA §165.101).
What kind of offense is a violation of the MPA? What kind offense is it to practice medicine in violation of the MPA? To practice medicine with financial harm?	**Misdemeanor class A; felony; jail felony** (MPA §165.103; MPA §165.152; MPA §165.153)
May you perform emergent surgery while drunk?	**No; emergency MIGHT be an exception** (MPA §165.1535).
If you have a contract with an impaired physician, can you avoid reporting him/her?	**No** (MPA §160.003-.004).
Can the board regulate advertising?	**No, except to prohibit false, misleading, or deceptive practice** (MPA §153.002).
Are "testimonials" allowable advertising?	**No** (Tex. Occ. Code §101.201).

Is it permitted to advertise board certification? Board eligibility?	**Certification, yes; not eligibility** (MPA §164.4).
What is a standing medical order?	**Physician order to institution, e.g., nursing home** (22 Tex. Admin. Code §193.2).
What is a standing delegation order? What are the requirements?	**Physician order for patient or population; signed, dated, in writing** (22 Tex. Admin. Code §193.2).
Who can a physician delegate to?	**Any qualified and properly trained person** (MPA §157.001).
Who can the physician delegate to administer dangerous drugs?	**Any qualified and trained person** (MPA §157.002).
Can a physician delegate to a midwife?	**Yes (e.g., eye prophylaxis)** (MPA §157.004).
Is a physician liable for the actions of a NP or PA?	**No, unless vicariously liable due to employment** (MPA §157.060).

What kind of name identification do PAs need?	**Name tag identifying themselves as a physician assistant** (Tex. Occ. Code §204.203).
What requirements exist for prescription for PAs and NPs?	**No schedule 2; maximum 90 days, no refills unless consultation with physician** (MPA §157.0511).
Which drug schedules can PAs and NPs prescribe? How many days? Can they give refills? Can they treat children? What ages?	**Schedules 3-5, 90 days, refill after consultation with physician; Yes, but children less than 2 years only after consultation with physician** (MPA §157.0511).
How many PA and NP equivalent FTEs can a physician supervise at maximum?	**3 FTEs** (22 Tex. Admin. Code §193.6(b)(3)).
Can CRNAs give all anesthetic drugs? Are they restricted to a particular MD?	**Yes; no, any MD** (MPA §157.058).
What authority do pharmacists have? Can they give immunizations? Where does the supervising physician have to be located geographically?	**Getting histories, ordering drug therapy-related tests, procedures, modifying drug therapy; yes; physician has to be able to be physically present daily** (MPA §157.101).

What can optometrists prescribe?	**Eye ointments** (Tex. Occ. Code §351.358).
Can anybody be a surgical assistant? Do they need a license?	**Yes; yes, if they identify themselves as licensed, otherwise, no** (Tex. Occ. Code §206.001 et seq.).
Can a physician delegate the taking of X-rays to noncertified technicians?	**Yes** (22 Tex. Admin. Code §194).
Can they do bone density? Nuclear tests? CT? Skull X-ray?	**Bone density, skull, spine, extremities, abdomen, chest; NOT CT, nuclear test, etc** (22 Tex. Admin. Code §194.5).
Do they need to be licensed or registered by the boards?	**Yes, they need registration** (22 Tex. Admin. Code §194.3).

Chapter 5

BUSINESS ORGANIZATIONS IN HEALTH CARE

What is the difference between a partnership and a limited liability partnership?	**The limited liability partnership can limit individual liability white partner A is liable for the acts of partner B** (Tex. Rev. Civ. Stat., art. 6123b-3.08(a) (1)).
Who can incorporate in Texas? Can physicians practice through corporations?	**Dentists, PT but NOT MD; MD cannot practice through corporation** (Texas Professional Corporation Act, Tex. Rev. Civ. Stat., art. 1528e).
Are there any corporations that can employ physicians?	**Yes, Certified Nonprofit Healthcare Corporation** (Tex. Occ. Code §162.001).

Who can grant such a certification?	**TMB** (Tex. Occ. Code §162.001).
What are 5 important characteristics of these entities?	**Must conduct scientific research, support education, improve capabilities to study and teach, deliver health care to the public, instruct public in medical science, public health** (Tex. Occ. Code §162.001(b)(1)(A)-(E)).
Can hospitals provide "physician guarantees"? How do the finances work?	**Physicians can contract with hospitals but are not employees; guarantees paid for availability, billing, etc** (Tex. Occ. Code §151.055).

Chapter 6

FRAUD AND ABUSE

Are there federal anti kickback laws?	**Yes** (42 USC §1320a-7b(b)).
What does the health care insurance portability and accountability act do to federal anti-kickback provisions?	**Applies to all federal health care insurances = all insurances** (Public Law. 104.191(1996)).
Do the anti-kickback laws apply only to Medicare and Medicaid?	**No** (Public Law. 104.191(1996)).
Does this law apply only to patient referrals?	**No** (Public Law. 104.191(1996)).
Does this law apply only to giving money as a kickback? Who is punished, giver or taker?	**No, any money or monetary value; both are punished** (42 USC §1320a-7b(b)).

What kind of crime is a violation of anti-kickback law, and what is the penalty for physicians and hospitals?	**Felony; up to $250,000 for individuals and $500,000 for institutions** (42 USC §1320a-7b(b)).
What are safe harbors? Give examples.	**Acts NOT in violation of anti-kickback regulation; e.g., space and equipment rental, sale of practice, discounts, etc** (Public L. No. 100-93, §14(1987)).
Are STARK laws federal?	**Yes** (42 USC §1395nn.).
What is a STARK law? Can you refer to family?	**Anti-self-referral law; no** (42 USC §1395nn.).
What is the difference between STARK 1 and STARK 2?	**Stark 1 applies to laboratories, Stark 2 to PT, OT services, etc** (42 USC §1395nn.).
What is the CIVIL FALSE CLAIMS act? Is it state or federal? How long has it been around? What does it prohibit?	**Submitting false claims to government for payment; federal law since War Between the States** (31 USC §§3729-3733).
Does Texas prohibit remuneration in exchange for referral volume?	**Yes, prohibition on the solicitation of patients** (Tex. Occ. Code §102.001).

Is it a crime to tamper with Texas Medical Board documents?	**Yes, class A misdemeanor** (Texas Penal Code §37.10).
Barratry—what is it? Is it illegal?	**Contacting prospective patients in attempts to solicit them; it is illegal** (Texas Penal Code §38.12).

Chapter 7

CREDENTIALING AND PEER REVIEW

Who can be part of a medical peer review committee?	**Physicians, health care workers, anybody in the hospital** (MPA §151.002).
Does physician competency include membership in societies, participation in education, participation in group plans?	**NO** (42 USC §11151).
Who makes rules (by laws) for hospitals?	**The governing body** (Texas Health & Safety Code §241.001 et seq.).
Can a hospital reject an orthopedist because he is a DO and not an MD?	**NO** (Texas Health & Safety Code §241.001 et seq.).
Can a hospital deny you privileges because you don't accept HMOs? Participate in other hospitals?	**NO** (Texas Health & Safety Code §241.1015).

Who makes the final decision in a hospital to grant or deny privileges to a physician?	**Governing body** (MPA §151.051).
Does the hospital have to get a report from the NPDB about physicians prior to granting privileges?	**Yes, initially and every 2 years; if they don't, they are liable** (42 USC §11101 et seq.).
How many days does the board have to give data to a hospital requesting it?	**15 days** (MPA §162.154).
How often must a physician update his core credentials? How many days does he have to provide corrections?	**Yearly; corrections within 30 days** (MPA §162.153).
Prior to the "first release" of his information, how many days does a physician have to review it?	**15 business days** (MPA §162.155).
If a physician's privileges will be suspended, does he/she have the right to due process?	**Yes** (Texas Health & Safety Code §241.101(c)).
How many days prior to hearing must they give the physician notification?	**30 days** (42 USC §11112(b)).
Do hospitals have to accept NPs and PAs?	**No** (Texas Health & Safety Code §241.105).

If they do, what are the hospital's responsibilities?	**Due process, fairness, appeal** (Texas Health & Safety Code §241.105).
Is the peer review file confidential?	**Yes, EXCEPT for possible civil rights violation and possible anti-trust violation** (MPA §160.007 (a)-(c)).
When must a hospital's medical peer review report actions taken against physicians to the TMB? to the HCQIA? to the NPDB?	**If action affects privileges for longer than 30 days or if physician surrenders privileges or if it affects membership; never, the TMB reports to NPDB** (MPA §160.002; 42 USC §11133(a)(I); 45 CFR §60.9).
How much time does the committee have to report to the TMB?	**15 days** (42 USC §11133(a)(I); 45 CFR §60.9).

Chapter 8

Consent, Patient Rights, and Advanced Directives

Is it good enough to get the signature for informed consent?	**No, actual informed consent must be achieved** (Tex. Civ. Prac. & Rem. Code, chapter 74, subchapter C).
Which procedures need "full disclosure" of LIST A and LIST B?	**Only list A** (Tex. Admin. Code §601.2).
Which procedures need additional "statutory consent"?	**Hysterectomy, radiation therapy, ECT** (Tex. Admin. Code §§601.4-.5, 601.8).
Is it the duty of the hospital or the physician to get consent?	**MD** (*Boney v. Mother Francis Hosp.*, 880 SW 2d 140 (Tex. App.—Tyler, writ denied)).

Which particular aspects of an informed consent if neglected can be grounds for a suit? Do you need to suffer damages to sue?	**Nondisclosure of risks, benefits, alternatives; yes** (Tex. Civ. Prac. & Rem. Code §74.101).
Is express consent required in an emergency?	**No, consent is implied** (Texas Health & Safety Code §773.008).
If arrested and suspected to be drunk, do the police need consent to check blood?	**No, consent is deemed to have been made, but consent can be expressly denied** (Tex. Trans. Code §724.011).
If anyone died in an accident, is consent needed to check blood?	**No** (Tex. Trans. Code §724.012-.013).
Who is a minor in Texas?	**Anybody less than 18 years of age who has not been emancipated** (Tex. Fam. Code §101.003(a)).
When can a minor petition the court NOT to be a minor?	**Age 16 when living independently and supporting self, age 17 when supporting self, managing conservator or guardian, Texas resident** (Tex. Fam. Code §31.001).
Can an uncle consent for a minor?	**Yes** (Tex. Fam. Code §32.001).

Can an educational institution consent for a minor?	**Yes (boarding school for example)** (Tex. Fam. Code §32.001).
Vaccinations: Is physician liable for damages by a required vaccination? Is physician liable for damages done by a disease that the parents denied vaccination for?	**No; no** (Texas Health & Safety Code §161.001).
Who is responsible to review a child's immunization record?	**Any physician; failure to do so has no consequence** (Texas Health & Safety Code §161.004).
What happens if a physician does not review record?	**Nothing** (Texas Health & Safety Code §161.004).
Do you need to consent to inform the authorities if you suspect child abuse or neglect?	**No** (Tex. Fam. Code §32.005).
In what instance can a child give consent?	**If on active duty, when restrictions of minor removed, for communicable disease, if pregnant for counseling, and addiction treatment** (Tex. Fam. Code §32.003).

Does the Consent to Medical Treatment Act apply to "incapacitated" individuals? Does it apply to psychiatry patients?	**Yes; yes, but not for patients in FREE-STANDING psychiatric hospitals** (Texas Health & Safety Code §313.001-.007).
Who can be a surrogate decision maker? What are the requirements?	**Spouse, adult child, majority of children, parents, or a person identified by patient before becoming incapacitated** (Texas Health & Safety Code §313.004).
Can surrogate decision maker consent to voluntary inpatient psych treatment? ECT treatment? Appoint another surrogate decision maker?	**Not psych treatment, not ECT, cannot appoint another decision maker** (Texas Health & Safety Code §313.003).
What are 3 examples of "advanced directive"?	**Directive to physician, out-of-hospital DNR, medical power of attorney** (Texas Health & Safety Code §166.031 et seq.; §166.081(6); §166.151 et seq.).
How many witnesses do you need, and what are the witness requirements for advanced directives?	**2 witnesses, one cannot be related, beneficiary, attending physician or hospital employee** (Texas Health & Safety Code §166.033).

Can a directive to a physician be oral or must it be in writing?	**Can be verbal and must be documented in chart with names of witnesses** (Texas Health & Safety Code §166.034).
Does an advanced directive have to be notarized?	**No** (Texas Health & Safety Code §166.032).
How many witnesses for an oral directive?	**2** (Texas Health & Safety Code §166.034).
How long is a directive good for?	**No limit, until revoked** (Texas Health & Safety Code §166.041-.043).
What are the 3 ways to revoke an advance directive?	**Written, oral, or VOID across the pages** (Texas Health & Safety Code §166.041-.043).
When a directive is orally revoked, what should the physician do with it?	**Destroy or write note on verbal revocation or write VOID across pages** (Texas Health & Safety Code §166.041-.043).
What happens if a physician disagrees with the directive given to him?	**Does not have to follow; can request ethics or medical committee with 48-hour notification for all parties** (Texas Health & Safety Code §166.046).

What is the transfer registry?	**Directory of physicians or hospitals willing to accept patients in transfer who have advanced directives** (Texas Health & Safety Code §166.053).
Is "mercy killing" allowed in Texas?	**No** (Texas Health & Safety Code §166.099).
Who must sign an "out-of-hospital DNR"? Can it be verbal? Are witnesses needed?	**Attending physician, patient, and two witnesses; yes/no; yes/no** (Texas Health & Safety Code §166.084).
What is the effect of an "out-of-hospital DNR"?	**Legally binding; patient's wishes written as a physician order** (Texas Health & Safety Code §166.081(6)).
If a patient's family disagrees with a patient's decision, what can they do?	**Must apply for temporary guardianship under Texas probate code** (Texas Health & Safety Code §166.088).
If you see a DNR device on a patient but have not seen the form, is that enough not to give treatment?	**Yes, DNR device is enough** (Texas Health & Safety Code §166.090).

Can an incompetent patient revoke their DNR?	**Yes** (Texas Health & Safety Code §166.091-.093).
Should this form accompany patients on transfers?	**Yes** (Texas Health & Safety Code §166.090).
What kind of treatment can the power of attorney NOT consent to?	**Admission to mental health institution, ECT, psychosurgery, abortion, neglect of minimal treatment (nutrition, hydration, comfort measures)** (Texas Health & Safety Code §166.152).
Does the power of attorney have an expiration date?	**No, unless specified** (Texas Health & Safety Code §166.152).
What happens if on the expiration date the patient is incompetent?	**It is continued until patient becomes competent again, then expires** (Texas Health & Safety Code §166.152).
Who cannot be the power of attorney?	**Principal health care provider or residential care provider or employee of those** (Texas Health & Safety Code §166.153).

Does the power of attorney have access to the patient's medical records?	**Yes** (Texas Health & Safety Code §166.157).
When can you withhold treatment to an infant?	**If chronically and irreversibly comatose or terminally ill and further treatment would be futile** (42 USC §5101 et seq.; 45 CFR §1340.15).
Does that include nutrition/hydration?	**NO; those must be continued** (45 CFR §1340.15(b)(2)).
Is the mental health directive an advanced directive act?	**Yes, but with differences** (Tex. Civ. Prac. & Rem. Code §137.001-.011).
What are the requirements for mental health directive? What are requirements for witnesses?	**Age 18 or not a legal minor, not incapacitated; 2 witnesses both of who cannot be related, beneficiaries, attending physician, or employees of hospital** (Tex. Civ. Prac. & Rem. Code §137.001-.011).
Does it have an expiration date?	**Yes, 3 years or until revoked** (Tex. Civ. Prac. & Rem. Code §137.002).

What happens if on the expiration date the patient is incapacitated?	**It continues until competent** (Tex. Civ. Prac. & Rem. Code §137.002).
When can you use restraints? When can you use behavioral measures?	**If there is danger of harm to self or others and other measures have failed; never** (42 CFR §482.13).

Chapter 9

Birth and Death

Does the donor have rights of a parent in artificial insemination? Does the husband?	**Donor NO, husband YES** (Tex. Fam. Code §151.101).
What prenatal maternal tests must a physician check?	**HIV, hepB, syphilis** (Texas Health & Safety Code §81.090).
How many times must a physician check them?	**Twice; upon first examination and on admission for delivery** (Texas Health & Safety Code §81.090).
Are these tests confidential and anonymous?	**Confidential; anonymous upon request** (Texas Health & Safety Code §81.090).

Does the physician have to tell the mother that he/she will do these tests? What if she wants anonymous testing?	**Yes, must inform but not specifically consent; if anonymous is wanted must refer patient to anonymous testing center; patient can refuse** (Texas Health & Safety Code §81.090).
If the tests are positive, what must the physician do?	**Refer for treatment, provide counseling, and provide information about diseases** (Texas Health & Safety Code §81.090).
How long does a physician have to keep test results?	**For 9 months** (Texas Health & Safety Code §81.090).
What institutions do not need licensing for birthing centers?	**Licensed hospitals, nursing homes, and ambulatory surgery centers** (Texas Health & Safety Code §224.001-.014).
What does the federal case *Roe v. Wade* say about abortion?	**Abortions are legal** (*Roe v. Wade*, 410 U.S. 113(1973)).
Under what circumstance can you perform a third trimester abortion in Texas?	**In emergency to save mother's life or if fetus has severe irreversible abnormality** (Texas Health & Safety Code §170.002).

After third-trimester abortion, how many days does the physician have to notify the Department of Health?	**30 days** (Texas Health & Safety Code §170.002).
What is the cut-off gestational age to do an abortion in the office?	**16 weeks** (Texas Health & Safety Code §171.001-.018).
What specific health risk must you inform the patient about during consent for abortion (4 categories)?	**Infection, hemorrhage, infertility, breast cancer** (Texas Health & Safety Code §171.001-.018).
What specific economic-related issues must you talk about?	**Medical assistance, father's liability for support** (Texas Health & Safety Code §171.001-.018).
Do you need to document in writing that you talked about these issues?	**Yes** (Texas Health & Safety Code §171.001-.018).
How long before the abortion must you tell them about the information?	**24 hours** (Texas Health & Safety Code §171.001-.018).
When can you perform an abortion on a minor? Can you do it without calling the parents?	**To save mother's life, court order, consent of parents; yes, only court ordered** (Tex. Fam. Code §33.001).

How much time prior to an abortion on a minor must you give notification to parents?	**48 hours** (Tex. Fam. Code §33.002(a)-(d)).
If they agree, can you do it earlier?	**Yes** (Tex. Fam. Code §33.002(a)-(d)).
What happens if you cannot find a parent?	**Mail certified letter 48 hours prior** (Tex. Fam. Code §33.002(a)-(d)).
Is there any way for a minor to have abortion without notifying the parents?	**Yes, can petition court if minor is mature, informed and notification may be harmful (abuse)** (Tex. Fam. Code §33.002-.004).
To perform emergency abortion on a minor, what must you do? What kind of form to fill out?	**Assure that it is necessary; notify TDDHS on prepared form** (Tex. Fam. Code §33.002).
What facility must be licensed to do abortions in Texas?	**If they do > 50/year** (Texas Health & Safety Code §245.010).
How often do abortion facilities have to report to the DPH?	**Yearly** (Texas Health & Safety Code §245.011).

Do the reports include the physician and patient names?	**NO, NEITHER** (Texas Health & Safety Code §245.011).
Can you force a physician to perform an abortion?	**No** (Tex. Occ. Code §103.001).
With what and for what do you have to treat all newborns?	**Ophthalmia neonatorum, tetracycline, erythromycin, or silver nitrate ophthalmic solution** (Texas Health & Safety Code §81.091; Tex. Admin. Code §97.136).
What genetic test must you do on all newborns? How many times? Who can do them? Can the parents object?	**PKU, galactose-1-phosphate uridyltransferase deficiency, sickling hemoglobinopathies, congenital adrenal hyperplasia, hypothyroidism; twice (at birth, 2 weeks later); physician or person attending birth; parents can object on religious grounds** (Texas Health & Safety Code §33.001-.038; 25 Tex. Admin. Code §37.51-.67).
Do hospitals have to give hearing test to all newborns?	**Yes** (Texas Health & Safety Code §47.001-.009).

Within what time period does insurance have to pay for hearing screen? When do they have to pay for follow-up care with regard to hearing?	**From birth until 30 days; up to 2 years of age** (Tex. Ins. Code §1367.103).
For what time period must an insurance cover a mother + newborn?	**48 hours normal delivery, 96 hours C-section; longer for complicated delivery** (Tex. Ins. Code §1366.055).
Who must review immunization history?	**Every physician** (Texas Health & Safety Code §81.023, 161.001-.005).
Until when must insurance pay for immunizations?	**Up to age 6** (Tex. Ins. Code §1367.053).
Who must submit the birth certificate?	**Physician, midwife, or person attending birth** (Texas Health & Safety Code §192.001-.027).
How many days do you have to submit?	**5 days** (Texas Health & Safety Code §192.001-.027).
What kind of crime is it if you don't submit it?	**Misdemeanor** (Texas Health & Safety Code §195.004).

What kind of crime is it if you submit false data?	**Felony third degree** (Texas Health & Safety Code §195.003).
How old or young must a baby be in order for a care provider to be able to take possession of an abandoned baby?	**60 days or less** (Tex. Fam. Code §262.302).
Can any money transaction be done during an adoption?	**Yes, only to cover expenses** (Texas Penal Code §25.08).
When is a person considered dead?	**Cardiac and respiratory functions cease to exist** (Texas Health & Safety Code §671.001-.002).
When is a ventilated person considered dead?	**Irreversible cessation of brain function** (Texas Health & Safety Code §671.001-.002).
What is the time of death for ventilated people?	**At time of determined brain death** (Texas Health & Safety Code §671.001-.002).
For your ventilated person, do you pronounce death before or after you turn off ventilator?	**Before** (Texas Health & Safety Code §671.001-.002).

Who can pronounce somebody dead?	**MD, PA, NP, RN** (Texas Health & Safety Code §671.001-.002).
Who must file the death certificate?	**Person in charge of interment** (Texas Health & Safety Code §193.001-.010).
How many days does the physician have to fill it out once it is given to him/her?	**5 days for MD to fill out medical portion, 10 days to send in death certificate** (Texas Health & Safety Code §193.001-.010).
Do fetuses require death certificates?	**If 350 grams or more or 20 week or older** (25 Tex. Admin. Code §§181.1, 181.7).
Sudden infant death syndrome (SIDS) applies to children ages _____ or younger.	**1 year** (Texas Health & Safety Code §673.001-.004).
In SIDS, is an autopsy required?	**Yes** (Texas Health & Safety Code §673.001-.004).
To whom and how fast must you report SIDS?	**To whom; Immediately** (Texas Health & Safety Code §673.001-.004).

Who pays for autopsy in SIDS?	**State** (Texas Health & Safety Code §673.001-.004).
If at the time of death the physician knows that the patient had a communicable disease, what must be done to the body?	**Report to TDSHS and tag body to indicate caution required due to communicable disease** (Tex. Admin. Code §9712).
The death of a child under _____ years must be reported.	**6 years** (Tex. Fam. Code §264.513-.515).
Whom do you report it to?	**Medical examiner or justice of the peace** (Tex. Fam. Code §264.513-.515).
What must they do?	**Hold inquest** (Tex. Fam. Code §264.513-.515).
How many days must have passed since the person was last seen in order to issue a "certificate of death by catastrophe"?	**10 days** (Texas Health & Safety Code §193.010).
Can you issue a certificate of death by catastrophe for a minor?	**Yes, with affidavit** (Texas Health & Safety Code §193.010).

What is the difference between an inquest and an autopsy?	**Inquest is investigation only into causes of death, autopsy is postmortem body examination** (Tex. Code Crim. Proc., art. 49.01).
Who does the inquest?	**Medical examiner or justice of the peace** (Tex. Code Crim. Proc., art. 49.01-.25).
Who has rights to consent to autopsy? In what order?	**Spouse, child, court or guardian, parent, next of kin, any person assuming custody** (Tex. Code Crim. Proc., art. 49.13).
If a person higher in hierarchy is not available, can the next person down consent?	**No** (Tex. Code Crim. Proc., art. 49.13).
If a member of a class (1 out of 4 children) consents but the other 3 do not agree, can they still do the autopsy?	**Yes, only one needs to consent** (Tex. Code Crim. Proc., art. 49.13).
What kind of crime is it if you assist in suicide and patient does not die? What if patient dies?	**Class C misdemeanor, if patient dies felony** (Texas Penal Code §22.08).
How many witnesses do you need to donate an organ if there is no will?	**2 witnesses, signed** (Texas Health & Safety Code §§692.003; 692.005).

Who has the power to donate the organ of a dead person?	**Spouse, child, parent, siblings, guardian, any authorized person** (Texas Health & Safety Code §§692.004; 692.010).
How can you revoke an organ gift? Do you have to tell the donee?	**Yes; no** (Texas Health & Safety Code §692.008).
Can you call the death and transplant the organ?	**Physician who determines death CANNOT participate in transplantation** (Texas Health & Safety Code §692.009).
At what age and how can a mentally retarded person donate a kidney?	**Age 12, by petitioning the district court** (Texas Health & Safety Code §613.002-.005).
Can a blood bank pay for blood? How? After how many days?	**Yes, by mailed check, 15 days after donation** (Tex. Civ. Prac. & Rem. Code §77.001-.004).

Chapter 10

Reporting Requirements in Suspected Abuse or Neglect

What is the duty of a medical professional when treating an adult with family violence? What languages to use?	**Duty to treat and provide information (and document that information was provided) in English and Spanish; no need to report** (Tex. Fam. Code §91.003).
Does the physician have to call the police?	**No, just inform victim of options** (Tex. Fam. Code §91.003).
What is the difference between a professional and a medical professional?	**Medical professional = MD; professional = anybody else, e.g., teacher** (Tex. Fam. Code §§261.001, 261.101(b)).

Reporting of child abuse? By whom? How fast? Can it be delayed? To whom (3 entities)?	**Report immediately but MUST be within 48 hours, cannot be delegated; to Texas Department of Protective and Regulatory Services, any law enforcement, Texas Youth Commission** (Tex. Fam. Code §§261.101, 261.103).
Will the TDPRS act on anonymous calls? Does it satisfy a professional duty to report?	**Yes, they will be acted upon but DO NOT satisfy duty to report** (Tex. Fam. Code §261.304).
How much time do professionals and medical professionals have to report the death of a child secondary to suspected abuse?	**48 hours** (Tex. Fam. Code §261.101-.110).
What kind of crime is lying in a report? Not submitting a report?	**State jail felony, misdemeanor class B** (Tex. Fam. Code §261.109).
Who must report nursing home abuse?	**Any person** (Texas Health & Safety Code §§242.122, 252.122).
Is the report verbal or written?	**Immediately verbally, written within 5 days** (Texas Health & Safety Code §§242.122(c), 252.122(c)).

What kind of offense is it NOT to report?	**Misdemeanor class A** (Texas Health & Safety Code §§242.131-.132, 252.130-.131).
Can the institution retaliate against a whistle-blower?	**No** (Texas Health & Safety Code §§242.122(b), 242.133, 252.122(b), 252.132).
When and within what time limit must nursing homes report resident deaths?	**Within 10 working days** (Texas Health & Safety Code §§242.134, 252.134).
How about if the resident just transferred to hospital within 24 hours and died?	**10 working days** (Texas Health & Safety Code §§242.134, 252.134).
Who is considered a child, elderly, or disabled person when talking about a criminal offense for injury of the above?	**14 year or younger, 65 or older or disabled older than 14** (Texas Penal Code §22.04).
Who is considered "elderly" when living at home?	**65 or older** (Tex. Hum. Res. Code §48.002).
What kind of offense is it if you do not report elderly abuse?	**Misdemeanor class A; false information class B** (Tex. Hum. Res. Code §48.052-.053).
Can a volunteer report abuse in a hospital, etc.?	**Yes** (Texas Health & Safety Code §161.132(a)).

Who is considered a mental health worker? Does that include priests?	**Social worker, addiction counselor, counselor, marriage therapist, clergy member, physician, psychologist; yes** (Tex. Civ. Prac. & Rem. Code §81.001).
Give definitions for 4 types of sexual contact	**Touching, deviate acts, intercourse, request for or suggestion of** (Tex. Civ. Prac. & Rem. Code §81.001).
What is sexual exploitation?	**Pattern for purposes of sexual gratification** (Tex. Civ. Prac. & Rem. Code §81.001).
What is therapeutic deception?	**Making patient believe it is part of treatment** (Tex. Civ. Prac. & Rem. Code §81.001).
What of the above questions is cause for action?	**All-contact, exploitation, deception** (Tex. Civ. Prac. & Rem. Code §81.002).
Is an employer liable for the sexual misconduct of a current or previous worker with a current or discharged or ex-patient?	**Yes, if employer has knowledge of past sexual exploitation or fails to inquire over the last five years of employment** (Tex. Civ. Prac. & Rem. Code §81.003(a)).

What are considered "emotional dependence"?	**Lack of emotional dependence of the patient on the therapist is a defense that can be raised in an action brought by a former patient** (Tex. Civ. Prac. & Rem. Code §81.005(b)).
Is it a defense that the contact was consented? Off the premises? Outside treatment sessions?	**No, no, no** (Tex. Civ. Prac. & Rem. Code §81.005(a)).
Who are the 2 agencies that should receive a report?	**State licensing board and prosecuting attorney of the county where the alleged offense occurred** (Tex. Civ. Prac. & Rem. Code §81.006(a) (1)-(2)).
When to report? What offense is failure to report?	**Within 30 days; misdemeanor** (Tex. Civ. Prac. & Rem. Code §§81.006(a), 81.006(e)).

Chapter 11

Disease Prevention, Control, and Reporting

If you are examining a patient with a communicable disease, what is your duty?	**Duty to instruct on prevention of reinfection, spread, and necessity to treat** (Texas Health & Safety Code §81.083(a)).
Who has to report communicable diseases?	**Physician, dentist, veterinarian, chiropractor** (Texas Health & Safety Code §81.042; 25 Tex. Admin. Code §97.2).
What sort of situations must be reported?	**Documented or suspected infection, exotic diseases, outbreaks** (Texas Health & Safety Code §81.042; 25 Tex. Admin. Code §97.2).

Can an employee in the office do the reporting?	**Yes, if designated by physician** (Texas Health & Safety Code §81.042; 25 Tex. Admin. Code §97.2).
If a physician reports a communicable disease, does the hospital also have to report it?	**Yes, both** (Texas Health & Safety Code §81.042; 25 Tex. Admin. Code §97.2).
If you treat a patient with a communicable disease that dies, what are your 2 responsibilities and within what time frame?	**Report death immediately and put toe tag on** (Texas Health & Safety Code §81.045; 25 Tex. Admin. Code §97.13).
What kind of crime is nonreporting?	**Class B misdemeanor** (Texas Health & Safety Code §81.049).
If you are a police officer, firefighter, etc., can you make somebody have an HIV test if you think you might have been exposed? Who do you call?	**Yes, request TDH** (Texas Health & Safety Code §§81.095, 81.050).
Is the police officer, etc., required to be tested himself/herself?	**No** (Texas Health & Safety Code §§81.095, 81.050).
If an employee is exposed, can the hospital check if the person is harboring an infective agent?	**Yes, to HepB, C, HIV** (Texas Health & Safety Code §§81.095, 81.050).
What diseases must they test for?	**Hep B, C, HIV** (Texas Health & Safety Code §§81.095, 81.050).

Do they need the patient's consent?	**No** (Texas Health & Safety Code §§81.095, 81.050).
Who must report occupational exposure? Does that include labs?	**Physicians, labs, health care workers; labs must report abnormal lead levels** (Texas Health & Safety Code §84.003).
What occupational exposure must be reported?	**Asbestosis, silicosis** (Texas Health & Safety Code §84.003).
Do you have to report birth defects?	**Yes** (Texas Health & Safety Code §87.001-.065).
Which diseases have to be reported immediately?	**Diphtheria, measles, anthrax, pertussis, hemophilus, plague, rabies, SARS, smallpox, yellow fever, etc** (25 Tex. Admin. Code chap. 97).
Which diseases must microbiology labs report immediately?	**Vancomycin-resistant staph, VRE, HIV, neisseria meningitis** (25 Tex. Admin. Code §§97.5, 97.132-.135).
Can you make somebody have HIV test? What are the 4 exceptions?	**No, unless during pregnancy, criminal proceedings, accidental exposure, consented** (Texas Health & Safety Code §81.001-.353).

What kind of crime is it if you force somebody to take an HIV test?	**Misdemeanor A** (Texas Health & Safety Code §81.001-.353).
Does HIV testing consent have to be written?	**No** (Texas Health & Safety Code §§81.105-.107, 81.095).
Do you have to sign an HIV consent if you have signed a consent for treatment?	**No** (Texas Health & Safety Code §§81.105-.107, 81.095).
Do you need consent for accidental exposure?	**No** (Texas Health & Safety Code §§81.105-.107, 81.095).
Does a physician have to contact the partner notification program if a patient is HIV positive and the physician suspects sexual activity?	**Yes** (Texas Health & Safety Code §81.051).
Can a health care worker with exudative lesions or weeping dermatitis participate in direct patient care or handling of medical equipment?	**No** (Texas Health & Safety Code §85.203).
If you are a health care worker that has HIV or hepB or HbeAg, can you perform invasive procedures that are "exposure-prone"? What are the 2 requirements?	**No, unless patient has been educated and has sought expert panel** (Texas Health & Safety Code §85.204-.205).

What if you do invasive procedures that are not exposure-prone?	**No need to inform** (Texas Health & Safety Code §85.204-.205).
Can you force rapists to undergo HIV and HepC tests?	**Yes** (25 Tex. Admin. Code §97.138).
Which neoplasm must be reported to the cancer registry?	**All** (Texas Health & Safety Code §82.001-.011; 25 Tex. Admin. Code §91.1-.12).
Which traumatic injuries must be reported? To whom? Who is responsible to report?	**Spinal cord, traumatic brain, anoxia including near-drowning; to TDH; physician** (Texas Health & Safety Code §92.002).
Do you have to report overdosing and gunshot wounds? How fast? Who are the 2 people who can report that?	**Yes; immediately; by physician or hospital administrator or official** (Texas Health & Safety Code §§161.041, 161.043, 161.042-.043).
What kind of offense is nonreporting?	**Misdemeanor** (Texas Health & Safety Code §§161.041, 161.043, 161.042-.043).

Chapter 12

Mental Health and Chemical Dependency

What is a "commitment order"?	**Court order for involuntary mental health admission** (Texas Health & Safety Code §571.003).
Who is considered an "adult" in order to proceed with voluntary psych admission?	**16 and over OR anybody who has ever been legally married** (Texas Health & Safety Code §572.001(a)).
What are the 3 types of involuntary psych admissions? Who can order them?	**Emergency or temporary detention, protective custody; they are court ordered** (Texas Health & Safety Code §§573.001-.026; 574.001; 574.021)
Does being on ETOH, senile, mental retardation, epilepsy constitute grounds to deny admission?	**No** (Texas Health & Safety Code §571.009).

When you are admitted involuntarily, when can a patient be forced to take psychoactive mediations (3 cases)?	**(1) a medication-related emergency, (2) under a court order, (3) patient is a ward and guardian consents** (Texas Health & Safety Code §575.101).
Do you need a separate court order to give psychoactive medications in addition to the court order for involuntary admission?	**Yes, you need 2 separate court orders** (Texas Health & Safety Code §574.103).
Do you need a physician order to put patient in restraints?	**Yes** (Texas Health & Safety Code §576.024).
When should you consider prescribing psychoactive medications?	**Medication emergency—threat to self or others** (Texas Health & Safety Code §574.103).
ECT may not be used in people less than _____ years of age	**16** (Texas Health & Safety Code §578.002).
Are there any exceptions?	**No** (Texas Health & Safety Code §578.002).

Can anyone, including courts, force somebody to have ECT without their written consent?	**No, ECT cannot be court ordered** (Texas Health & Safety Code §578.003).
How often do you need consent for ECT?	**Before every single treatment** (Texas Health & Safety Code §578.003).
How about people > 65 years of age, who must sign for ECT?	**Patient and 2 physicians** (Texas Health & Safety Code §578.003).
Can psychiatry hospitals employees' pay be based on # of admissions, length of stay, calls to referring sources?	**No** (Texas Health & Safety Code §164.005).
Can psychiatry hospitals "guarantee" a cure on advertising?	**No** (Texas Health & Safety Code §164.010).
Can psychiatry hospitals solicit information about patients' confidential records to solicit them for services?	**No** (Texas Health & Safety Code §164.010).
Can a physician send a patient directly to psychiatry hospital? Do they have to first get insurance approval?	**Yes; no** (Texas Health & Safety Code §164.007).

How long is a mental health directive valid for?	**3 years or earlier if revoked** (Tex. Civ. Prac. & Rem. Code §137.002).
Does a mental health directive suffice to allow ECT treatment?	**Yes, it is considered a prior consent** (Texas Health & Safety Code §578.003).
Does Texas have "duty to warn" for mentally-ill patients? Is this breach of confidentiality	**Texas does NOT have duty to warn, it IS a breach of confidentiality** (*Thapar v. Zezullea*, 994, SW 2d 635, 638 (Tex. 1999)).
Can patient refuse mental health treatment after admission?	**If they are voluntarily admitted, yes; if involuntarily, no, with court order** (Texas Health & Safety Code §576.021).

Chapter 13

Emergency Medical Treatment and Hospital Transfers

Who does EMTALA apply to?	**Hospitals participating in Medicare** (42 USC §1395 dd(a); 42 CFR §489.24(a)).
What is considered "campus"?	**250 yards from ER** (42 CFR §489.24(b)).
What 4 places constitute "coming" to the ER?	**In hospital-owned ambulance or air transport, or patient is in ER or in hospital requesting ER consultation** (42 CFR §489.24(b)).
If an ambulance despite being told that the hospital is on diversion comes to the ER, can you send them away?	**No, patient HAS TO BE SEEN** (42 CFR §489.24(b)).

Is pregnancy a medical emergency?	**No, except for complications and labor** (42 CFR §489.24(b)).
Under EMTALA, what MUST a hospital provide?	**Medical screening** (42 USC §489.24(a)).
Is it enough to log in or triage the patient?	**No** (42 USC §489.24(a)).
Can you delay treatment in order to check insurance? Get pre-approval?	**No** (42 USC §1395 dd(h); 42 CFR §489.24(d)(4)).
Can you provide different levels of care based on insurance?	**No** (42. USC §489.24(a)).
Can a PA or NP provide the EMTALA required screening?	**Yes** (42 USC §489.24(a)).
Does admitting the patient for treatment satisfy EMTALA requirements?	**No** (42 CFR §489.24(d)(2)).
If patient refuses treatment, does that satisfy EMTALA? What is the appropriate protocol?	**Yes; has to be informed of potential dangers** (42 USC §§1395dd(b)(2), 1395dd(b)(3); 42 CFR §§489.24(d)(3), 489.24(d)(5)).

If a physician is not available to determine if transfer is necessary, who else can do it? What is required?	**PA, NP, RN, other qualified person after consultation with MD** (42 USC §1395dd(c); 42 CFR §489.24(c)).
Do you have to send medical records?	**Yes** (42 USC §1395dd(c); 42 CFR §489.24(e)(2)).
Can you transfer because on-call physician did not show up? What must you do?	**Yes; record name and address of physician who did not show up** (42 CFR §489.24(j)).
Can a specialized hospital (e.g., burn unit) refuse a transfer because "they are full"?	**No, if they have EVER accepted patients before and made room for them** (42 USC §1395dd(g); 42 CFR §489.24(f)).
How many years must you keep records of patient transfers?	**5 years** (42. USC §§1395cc(a) (1) (I), 1395cc(N) (iii); 42 CFR §§489.20(g), 489.20(r)).
Do hospitals need to keep on-call lists?	**Yes** (42 CFR §489.24(j)).
Can you do elective surgery when you are on call?	**Yes** (42 CFR §489.24(j)).

Can on-call physician refuse to show up?	**No, only in circumstances beyond his control** (42 CFR §489.24(j)).
What are the 3 penalties for hospitals and physicians for violation of EMTALA? What is the maximum damage?	**Civil money penalties, termination of provider agreement, civil action. Up to $50,000 per violation ($25,000 for < 100 beds)** (42 USC §1395dd(d)(1)(A); 42 CFR §§489.20(1), 489.24(g), 489.53(b)(1); 42 USC §1395dd(d)(2)).
Can a patient initiate his/her own transfer?	**Yes** (42 USC §1395dd(c); 42 CFR §489.24(e)).

Chapter 14

NUMBERS, DATES, TIMES TO REMEMBER

How many people on the board?	**19.**
How many MDs/DOs?	**12.**
How many lay persons?	**7.**
How often does the police run a check on physicians?	**1 x / month.**
How often does the TMB put out reports?	**2 x / year.**
How many years of postgraduate training to apply for full license?	**1.**
If a resident does not show up to begin his training, how many days does the program director have to report that to the board?	**7.**
Institutional permit: how many months for initial license? How many renewals? How many months for each renewal?	**14 months; 7; 12 months.**

Physician-in-training permit: how many months for initial license? How many renewals? How many months for each renewal?	**18 months; 6; 18 months.**
How often do you register your license?	**Every 2 years.**
How many days prior to expiration of your license does the board notify you?	**30.**
How many days after expiration are you considered practicing without a license?	**30.**
How many days after expiration is license canceled?	**365.**
How many CMEs per year?	**24.**
How many category 1 CMEs per year?	**12.**
How many ethics?	**1.**
How many can be from volunteering?	**6.**
How many CMEs can you carry forward?	**48.**
How many CMEs retroactively?	**24.**
How often must the board give update to all participants in a complaint?	**Every 3 months**
How much time do insurances have to report malpractice to the board?	**30 days.**

If disciplinary action is taken by the board, how much time to report to the hospital verbally? In writing? To the NPDB?	**Verbally immediately to hospitals on first working day; in writing to all hospitals and agencies within 30 days.**
How much time to report court reports to the board?	30 days.
How many malpractice claims in what time frame to trigger board investigation?	3 within 5 years.
How many people from the board to emergency suspend license?	3.
How many days does a physician have to file appeal to a board decision? Which county?	30 days; Travis County.
How soon and how often can you file for reinstatement of a license?	After one year; once a year.
Maximum administrative penalty by board? By attorney general?	$5000 per violation; $1000 per violation.
How much time to pay it?	30 days.
How many days can NPs and PAs prescribe? How many refills? For patients how old?	30 days, no refills; older than 2 years.
How many PA equivalents can an MD supervise?	3 FTEs.

TEXAS JURISPRUDENCE STUDY GUIDE

What percentage of random charts of the PA must the physician review?	**10%.**
How far can secondary practice sites be located from primary?	**60 miles.**
How many days does board have to give information to requesting hospitals?	**15 business days.**
How many days do you have to correct changes in your profile?	**30 days.**
How many days do you get to review your data the FIRST time the board releases it?	**15 business days.**
How often does a physician have to resubmit his core data if there were no changes?	**Once a year.**
How many days before hospital hearing must a physician be notified?	**30 days.**
A suspension in the hospital must be reported if it lasts for how long? Within what time must it be reported?	**More than 30 days; 15 days.**
Until what age is one considered a minor?	**18 years.**
How many witnesses do you need for advanced directive? For verbal directive to physician? For out-of-hospital DNR?	**2; 2; 2.**
How many witnesses for a mental health directive?	**2.**

How long until mental health directive expires? How long until medical directives expire?	**3 years; no limit.**
How many days does a physician have to give records to patient? Hospital? Attorney?	**15 business days; 15 business days; 45 days.**
How many days does patient have to pay fees for requested records?	**10 days.**
What are the fees for copied records? Postage or not?	**$25 for first 20 pages, then 15¢ per page plus postage.**
How many years must a physician keep records for adults? For minors? From what age?	**7 years; 7 years or age 21.**
How many years must hospitals keep records for adults? For minors? From what age?	**10 years; 10 years or 20th birthday.**
How many days does a hospital have to send itemized bill if requested?	**30 business days.**
What is the economic cap on noneconomic damages in Texas per defendant/claimant?	**$250,000.**
How long is the statute of limitations for adults? Minors?	**2 years; 2 years from age 18.**
When must a claimant send a letter, and by how long can he/she extend the statute of limitations?	**Within 60 days; extends by 75 days.**
How many yards from ER is considered campus?	**250 yards.**

How many years must you keep records of transferred patients?	**5 years.**
What is the maximum monetary penalty for a hospital violating EMTALA?	**$50,000, $25,000 if < 100 beds.**
How long do physicians have to keep screening test records from the first visit of a pregnant woman?	**9 months.**
How many days does a physician have to notify the DPS of a third trimester abortion?	**30 days.**
What is the cut-off gestational age for office-based abortions?	**16 weeks.**
How long prior to abortion must you give the woman information on abortion (verbal/written)?	**24 hours.**
How much time prior to abortion must parents of a minor be notified?	**48 hours.**
How many abortions per year make you an abortion facility that must be licensed?	**50.**
How often does licensed abortion facility submit records to TSDHS?	**Yearly.**
How many times must you check newborn for genetic disorders?	**2.**
How long can a mother + newborn stay in the hospital paid by insurance after birth with vaginal delivery/cesarean section?	**48 hours/96 hours.**

TEXAS JURISPRUDENCE STUDY GUIDE

Until when must an insurance pay for hearing screening? Follow-up hearing screening?	**30 days; 2 years.**
Until when must insurance pay for immunizations?	**6 years.**
How many days do you have to submit birth certificate?	**5 days.**
After what age can you take possession of an abandoned baby?	**60 days or less.**
How many days does the funeral director have to file death certificate?	**10 days.**
How many days does the physician have to fill out death certificate?	**5 days.**
Over what weight must a death certificate be filled out for a fetus?	**350 grams.**
If weight is not known, over what gestational age?	**20 weeks.**
SIDS is for children of less than what age?	**1 year.**
When do you have to report SIDS?	**Immediately.**
Death of a child of what age or younger must be reported to the medical examiner? Within what time frame?	**6 years, immediately.**
How many days after catastrophe to get "certificate of death by catastrophe"?	**10 days.**

TEXAS JURISPRUDENCE STUDY GUIDE

If a patient dies within how many hours of admission must an inquest be ordered?	**24 hours.**
A mentally retarded person of what age can donate a kidney if the guardian petitions the court?	**12 years.**
After how many days can a blood bank pay for blood donation?	**15 days.**
A person older than what age can voluntarily commit self to psychiatry?	**16 years.**
How often do private psychiatry hospitals file reports?	**Yearly.**
What age do you have to be to get ECT?	**16.**
How often do you renew DEA license? DPS license?	**Every 3 years; yearly.**
How many days to you have to inform the DPS of change in information?	**7.**
How many days of pills can a patient get of schedule 2-5 when discharged from the hospital?	**7.**
How many days to send written prescription to pharmacy of schedule 2 drug?	**7.**
How long is a schedule 2 script valid? How many refills? Schedule 3-5 valid? Refills? Dangerous drugs valid? Refills?	**7 days; no refills; 6 months; 5 refills; unlimited; unlimited.**

TEXAS JURISPRUDENCE STUDY GUIDE

How often do you need to do inventory on your drugs?	**Every 2 years.**
How often do you have to register with the board and pay a fee to administer anesthesia?	**Every 2 years.**
How many days do you have to report an office-based anesthesia complication?	**15 days.**
How much time do you have to report a death from communicable disease?	**Immediately.**
How much time to report a gunshot wound?	**Immediately.**
What is the monetary penalty for violation of anti-kickback laws for physicians? Hospitals?	**$25,000-$250,000 / $50,000-$500,000.**
How much time does a physician have to report child abuse?	**Immediately; 48 hours in writing.**
How much time does a professional (not medical professional) have to report child abuse?	**48 hours.**
How much time do professionals/physicians have to report death of a child secondary to abuse?	**48 hours.**
How much time do you have to report nursing home abuse verbally? In writing?	**Immediately; 5 days.**
If a nursing home resident dies after transfer to a hospital, within what time frame must be reported?	**24 hours.**

How much time does the nursing home have to report elderly death?	**10 days after the end of the month of death.**
What are the age limits to consider abuse a criminal offense?	**14 or younger, 65 or older; older than 14 and disabled.**

The information in this book was compiled to the best of our abilities and its purpose is for studying and not to base medical or legal decisions on.

Made in United States
Orlando, FL
19 May 2023